FOWL LAN~~~

TWEENAGE WASTELAND

BRIAN GORDON

Rocketship Entertainment, LLC
rocketshipent.com

Tom Akel, CEO & Publisher • **Rob Feldman,** CTO • **Jeanmarie McNeely,** CFO
Brandon Freeberg, Dir. of Campaign Mgmt. • **Phil Smith,** Art Director • **Aram Alekyan,** Designer
Jimmy Deoquino, Designer • **Jed Keith,** Social Media • **Jerrod Clark,** Publicity

For my ducklings,
Max, Phoebe, Ike and Millie,
and for my sweet girl, Cat.
I love you all so much.
Thanks for all the inspiration
and for putting up with me.

B. Gordon

INTRODUCTION

"May you live in interesting times" is an old expression that sounds like a blessing but meant as a curse—the understanding being that uninteresting times are marked by tranquility, while interesting times are full of turmoil and constant upheaval.

We were warned well ahead of time that the tween and teen years would be a ridiculous shit-show, and yet we continued raising them in spite of this knowledge. Technically, yes, it IS the law, but we also loved them. And hey, maybe they would be the exception to the rule?

Well, no. Sadly all the cliches are true. All the crying, drama, and ceaseless arguing arrived as promised—and that was just me. Not to be outdone, the kids are doing their best to give as good as they get. It's loads of fun.

To add to the challenge, each of our four kids are challenging (read: torturing) us in their own unique and contradictory ways. At any given moment, one of our kids may have taken a vow of silence, while another speaks only in screams. We've simultaneously faced resentment for somehow holding one back from their true scholastic potential, while the others are furious that we ask that they complete any of their schoolwork.

Just to make things extra-interesting, all of this drama happened to kick off around the same time as the Covid lockdowns. As if living with four hormonal kids wasn't challenging enough, fate decided to lock us indoors together for a couple years. For the record, I've excluded nearly all my quarantine-related cartoons from this collection as a courtesy to the reader. I'm as nostalgic as the next guy, but no one needs a reminder of the days when we thought we had to bleach our groceries before hunting and gathering for toilet paper.

In collecting these cartoons, I'm reminded of a mom and her teenage daughter who came up to me outside of a sandwich shop shortly after my first child was born. It was the first time I had left the house since he was born and I was sleep-deprived, demoralized and questioning if I was even up to the task of being a parent.

She fawned over him for a moment and then added bitterly "Enjoy this time. It only gets worse." I remain dumbstruck by her assholery. Not only was this the exact-wrong pep talk I needed at the time, but in hindsight, she was dead wrong. As hard as the kids are now, I would never trade this time for the days of sleepless nights and getting thrown up on after every meal.

So, while this book is dedicated to my family, who, despite all my teasing, I love with every ounce of my being, I also dedicate this book to that woman. I can only hope you had a dozen more babies since the day we met, and I pray they are all interesting as fuck.

To everyone else, I hope you get a laugh and maybe some comfort from this collection of cartoons. If I can do this, surely you can, too.

(I *can* do this, right??)

B. Gordon

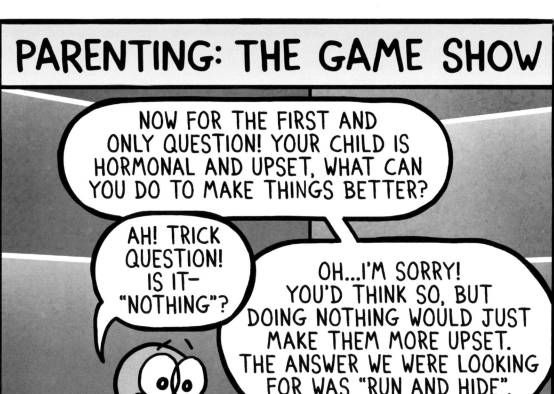

IT'S A PARENT'S JOB TO BE ON THE LOOKOUT FOR ANY HIDDEN TALENTS YOUR CHILDREN MAY HAVE—

YOU'RE JUST NEVER, EVER ALLOWED TO MENTION IT TO THEM.

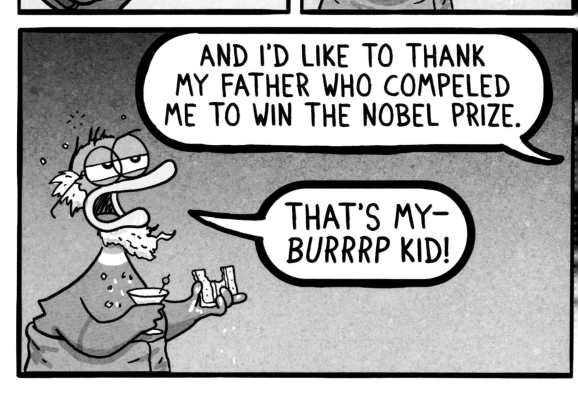

WHO KNEW I'D EVER LONG FOR THE DAYS WHEN THE KIDS DIDN'T GIVE A SHIT WHAT THEY LOOKED LIKE.

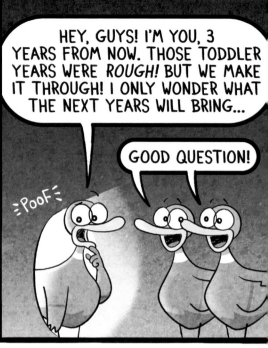

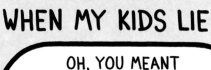

TALKING WITH MY CHILDREN: A BRIEF TIMELINE

WAYS I TORTURE MY CHILDREN #4,326

OUR UNEXPECTED EMOTIONS AFTER CHECKING OUT NEXT YEAR'S CLASSES FOR THE KIDS

WHO'S HAPPIER?

A CHILDREN'S GUIDE TO CLOTHES MANAGEMENT AND STORAGE

THE CLOTHES BASKET

WHERE CLOTHES ARE KEPT AFTER BEING CLEANED.

THE FLOOR

WHERE CLOTHES GO WHEN THEY'RE DIRTY.

HAMPER & CLOSET

?????

Prints!

Just one last note of thanks to everyone who has supported my
work over the years, both on Tinyview.com and on Patreon.
It's been my joy and privledge to share my stuggles, frustrations and more
than a couple mushy moments with you all. Without your help I would have
been out of a job long, long ago.

Much love, Brian

Brian Gordon began drawing FOWL LANGUAGE back in 2013 as a fun (and often profane) way to vent his frustrations over the day-to-day challenges of being a parent to two small children. Over the years, his super-relatable comics have become a viral Internet sensation, shared regularly by millions of overworked parents all over the world! He's since remarried and with two more ducks in his flock, the material just keeps on coming.

Brian's also the creator behind the mystery comic series FRANKIE FEARLESS— you can read both comics (as well as many others) at tinyview.com or on the TinyView app.

And of course, you'll find him on all your favorite social media outlets—and let's face it, he's way more fun to read than your cousin's political posts.